HOTSPOTS

IRELAND
A DIVIDED COUNTRY

JOHN LEWIS

A GLOUCESTER PRESS BOOK

Contents

The Irish "troubles" have their roots in history. A mix of ethnic and religious groups has emerged in Ireland, containing people whose vision of the future has differed. This has created friction which has often led to violence. The original settlers of Ireland — the Celts or "native Irish" — had their own distinct society, based on tribal custom and overlaid by Catholicism. Disrupted but not destroyed by the Normans in the 12th century, this society evolved in a different way from that elsewhere in Britain.

Protestant monarchs of England intervened in Ireland when they saw it as a potential base to be used by their Catholic enemies in Europe. Irish society was undermined and, especially in the northern province of Ulster, displaced. At the same time, Catholicism was suppressed, leading to attempts by the native Irish to fight back. Violence was used, although by the 19th century more peaceful, constitutional methods were also being followed, through the British parliament.

The idea of an Irish parliament responsible for Irish affairs – "Home Rule" – became a possibility in the early years of the 20th century and this alienated the Protestants in the north. They felt threatened by the Catholic majority in the island as a whole. Both sides reacted with violence of their own. These violent outbursts were reduced but not eradicated when Ireland was split in 1921 after a successful guerrilla campaign against the British in the south by the Irish Republican Army (IRA).

The emergence of the Irish Free State (later the Irish Republic) and the creation of the separate province of Northern Ireland, still part of the United Kingdom, perpetuated friction. In 1969, as Catholics and Protestants clashed in the North, the British Army was deployed to keep them apart. A new round of "troubles" began.

This has been going on for 20 years, fuelled by extremist groups on both sides. The violence has been "contained" by the British Army and the Royal Ulster Constabulary. But, until a political solution acceptable to all factions is introduced, people will continue to die. The Anglo-Irish Agreement of November 1985 may offer the beginning of such a solution, but the road to peace is long. History is not easy to forget.

◁ A mural, painted on the gable-end of a row of terraced houses in Belfast, reflects the nationalistic view of Irish history: the hand, representing Britain, squeezing and dividing the country in its iron grip. This is not a view shared by all.

The Nature of the Problem

Ireland as a whole is not a country at war. But it is a troubled one, split by an imposed border and subject to localized violence, particularly in the North. To understand why, we must examine Irish history.

On the morning of Sunday, 8 November 1987, the people of Enniskillen, a small town in County Fermanagh, Northern Ireland, gathered at their local war memorial to remember the dead of two world wars. It was an act repeated in cities, towns and villages throughout Great Britain. But, on this particular Remembrance Sunday, Enniskillen was to suffer new horror and loss.

At 10.45am, as the crowds were gathering and the military band was tuning up, a 30-pound bomb exploded without warning. It was planted by a group known as the Provisional IRA (Irish Republican Army) in the St Michael's Reading Rooms, a former school close to the war memorial. The wall of the building blew outwards, showering civilian onlookers with concrete and bricks. Eleven people, many of them elderly, but including a young trainee nurse, were killed and 61 more innocent bystanders were injured.

The bombing was immediately and universally condemned. Margaret Thatcher, Prime Minister of Great Britain, called it "cruel and callous"; the Reverend Ian Paisley, a Protestant political and religious leader in Northern Ireland, denounced it as a "diabolical deed by hell-inspired monsters". Even the Soviet news agency *Tass*

uncharacteristically described it as "a terrorist atrocity". *Sinn Fein* ("Ourselves Alone"), the political mouthpiece of the IRA, tried to excuse the action by saying that it was aimed at "Crown Forces" in Northern Ireland (the Royal Ulster Constabulary and the British Army), not at civilians, but their leader, Gerry Adams, still felt obliged to express regret at the high casualty figures. By any standards, it was a shocking event.

It would be wrong to imagine that such incidents are normal, everyday occurrences in Ireland. The vast majority of Irish people are peace-loving members of an ordered democratic society, whether they live north or south of the border in their divided country. But Enniskillen fits into a pattern of violence, perpetrated by a very small and unrepresentative minority of the population, which makes Ireland a troubled state. Since 1969, more than 500 British Army soldiers, 300 members of the Royal Ulster Constabulary and 2,000 civilians have been killed in Northern Ireland.

The bombs, bullets and beatings, used by extremist organizations intent on forcing their opponents to adopt different policies or beliefs, have sadly affected an entire generation. People have grown up in an atmosphere of violence. The children who experienced the beginning of the latest crisis, that began in the late 1960s, are now full-grown, with children of their own. In 1987 British soldiers, who had not even been born when that round of "troubles" began, went out on the streets of Belfast.

△ The funeral of Mary Wilson, a trainee nurse – just one of the innocent victims killed in Enniskillen. The town's war memorial is on the left, with the rubble of the bomb explosion to the right.

▽ Members of a Protestant paramilitary group, each wearing a "uniform" of dark glasses, beret and anorak, march through the streets of Belfast. Such groups, on both sides of the religious divide, illustrate the kind of deep rooted hatred that exists in Northern Ireland.

◁ The Reverend Ian Paisley, an outspoken "Loyalist", determined to maintain links with Britain. He represents the more extreme Protestant Irish people, personifying their fears.

A pattern of violence

During the twenty years up to 1989, other incidents as shocking as Enniskillen have taken place on a regular basis. On August Bank Holiday Monday, 27 August 1979, Earl Mountbatten of Burma, cousin to the British Queen and a widely respected military commander from the Second World War, was murdered.

Mountbatten and members of his family were sailing off the coast of the Irish Republic (Southern Ireland) when they and their boat were blown to pieces.

Later the same day, 18 British soldiers – members of the Parachute Regiment and the Queen's Own Highlanders – were killed in an ambush at Warrenpoint in Northern Ireland.

Other incidents spring to mind. On 17 December 1983 the prestigious London store, Harrods of Knightsbridge, was devastated by a bomb which killed five people. Less than a year later, on 12 October 1984, the Grand Hotel in Brighton, England, was badly damaged and members of the ruling Conservative government killed and injured.

Perhaps most shocking of all, on 19 March 1988, two British Army corporals, belonging to the Royal Signals stationed in Northern Ireland, were murdered in horrific and very public circumstances. As the car in which they were travelling blundered into an IRA funeral on the

▽ The scene outside Harrods department store, in London, after an IRA bomb explosion on 17 December 1983, in which five people were killed.

▷ The Grand Hotel in Brighton after the IRA tried to kill the British Prime Minister Margaret Thatcher, on 12 October 1984.

Andersonstown Road in Belfast, the men were dragged out, beaten and eventually shot, all under the full glare of television cameras. It was a brutal and seemingly senseless act of uncontrolled mob violence.

The roots of the problem

But to dismiss anything as senseless runs the risk of ignoring it, sweeping it under the carpet of our minds because there appears to be no solution. If that solution is to be found and Ireland restored to peace throughout its length and breadth, an understanding of why such incidents occur at all is essential. It is out of such understanding – something that has been sadly lacking in Irish history – that tolerance will grow.

It is therefore to that history that we must turn; it is there that the roots of the present-day troubles lie, buried in the mists of Irish nationalism and an 800-year record of British interference and rule.

Out of this mix have grown religious, cultural and political divisions. All of these divisions are reflected in the current crisis in Northern Ireland, itself a living reminder of past problems and unsatisfactory solutions. It is a complex story, but one that must be told.

The present situation

The people of Ireland fall into two main religious groups: Catholics and Protestants. Most of the Protestants live in the North, where they greatly outnumber the Catholics. By contrast, the population in the South – the Republic – is overwhelmingly Catholic.

▽ William of Orange, shown with sword drawn on horseback, supervises his forces at the Battle of the Boyne in July 1690. His victory in this battle firmly established British rule in Ireland. This led to a period known as the Anglican Ascendancy, in which the native Catholic population was deliberately excluded from society at every level. The victory is still celebrated annually by the Protestants in Northern Ireland.

Irish Independence

Ireland has been subject to British interference and rule for over 800 years. During that time, the Catholic Irish have been suppressed, displaced by Protestant settlers and forced to fight for their independence. Their success has been only partial.

△ Members of the Loyalist "Orange Order" in Portadown, Northern Ireland.

The British, or more accurately the Normans, first showed an active interest in Irish affairs in 1169, when Richard FitzGilbert de Clare ("Strongbow") landed in Ireland with a small army. He arrived with the blessing of King Henry II of England, ordered by the Pope to extend to the "barbarous" people of Ireland "the Christian faith".

Ireland was neither barbarous nor unchristian. Instead, Strongbow found a distinct Celtic (or Gaelic) society with a tradition of Christianity dating back 700 years to the time

◁ A romanticized view of the marriage of the Norman army leader Richard FitzGilbert de Clare ("Strongbow"), in the late 12th century.

Strongbow led a small Norman army into Ireland in 1169, starting a tradition of interference from "across the water" that was to last for over 800 years. His arrival was a portent of things to come.

of St Patrick. The Irish may have drifted away from the teachings of Rome, and they were certainly no strangers to violence, but they had their own language, culture and laws. As the Normans settled in the country, they found Gaelic ways appealing and did little to destroy them.

The seeds of discontent

Destruction of the traditional Irish lifestyle began in the 16th and 17th centuries. Newly Protestant Tudor and Stuart monarchs, fearful that Catholic enemies might use Ireland as a base from which to attack Britain, imposed a stricter rule. By the 1540s laws had been passed to make the Gaelic language illegal, the Latin Mass had been banned and lands taken away from anyone – Norman and native Irish – who refused to conform.

In 1609, after a rebellion by Hugh O'Neill of Ulster, in the north of Ireland, a policy of "plantation" (granting confiscated land to Protestant settlers who would be loyal to Britain) was introduced. By the 1620s Ulster contained 20,000 "planters", displacing Catholic farmers who were pushed west, into the wilds of Connaught.

The first bloodshed

This anti-Catholic policy bred resentment on several fronts. The Norman-Irish were fearful that their lands would be lost, the native Irish were forced to accept an alien culture, and the Catholic clergy were desperate to see their religion survive. Together, they rebelled in 1641, turning on the planters and massacring some 12,000. It was an action the Protestants of Ulster were never to forget, producing a fear of Catholic domination that is still very apparent today.

Revenge came in 1649 when Oliver Cromwell, leader of the victorious Parliamentarians in the English Civil War – a war in which the Irish Catholics had unfortunately supported the King – landed in Ireland to extend his rule by terror. Yet another element was added to Irish history – a fear among the Catholics of British brutality.

This was reinforced 40 years later when the Catholics again backed the losing side in a British quarrel – James II instead of William of Orange. The Protestants in the North supported William. They held Londonderry against James for seven months after 13 Apprentice Boys slammed the gates in the face of his army – and their victory was complete after the Battle of the Boyne in July 1690. Both events continue to be celebrated annually in the North.

△ Robert Emmet, leader of an abortive attack on Dublin Castle against British rule, proclaiming the Irish Republic in 1803. Like many Irish patriots, Emmet was found guilty of treason and publicly hanged. He became a symbol of Irish nationalism, inspiring a host of future activists.

Catholics lose their rights

"King Billy's" victory ushered in a period known as the Anglican Ascendancy during which British rule was firmly established. It was backed by "Penal Laws" which made it illegal for Irish Catholics to purchase or inherit land, to vote or to sit in either the Dublin or London parliaments. Further unrest was inevitable, particularly towards the end of the 18th century when new and attractive ideas of freedom and tolerance were being expressed through the American and French Revolutions. The first political nationalistic movements were in fact those begun by Protestant colonists, in response to the American Revolution.

In 1791 Wolfe Tone, an Anglican radical, founded the Society of United Irishmen and, in May 1798, they rose in revolt. The British, at war with France, recognized the danger of enemy interference. They put down the revolt with cruel force, then ensured direct rule of Ireland in 1801, abolishing the Irish parliament and centralizing the government in London. Ordinary Irish people were unaffected. They had no right to vote. Their only attempt at rebellion, led by Robert Emmet in 1803, was a disaster. The transfer of the government to England meant, however, that from now on the problems of Ireland could not be ignored by the British parliament.

△ Wolfe Tone, leader of the 1798 uprising in Ireland, a believer in ideas of freedom, spreading from Europe.

The fight for freedom begins

This was shown in 1829 when Daniel O'Connell, a Catholic Irish lawyer, gathered enough support through his Catholic Association of Ireland to force the British to grant Catholic Emancipation (freedom to worship, own land and vote). By this time nationalist sentiment was more widespread and better organized than it had ever been before.

O'Connell entered parliament and, with a group of like-minded Irish politicians, turned his attention to calls for an end to the Act of Union. Despite continued support from the ordinary Irish people, he made little headway.

Frustration at this failure, coupled to O'Connell's refusal to do anything illegal to further his cause, led to the emergence of a more radical group, known as the Young Irelanders. Led by William Smith O'Brien, they tried to organize a rebellion in Ireland against British rule. In July 1848, at the head of a small group of half-starved peasants, O'Brien was ignominiously defeated by only 46 members of the Irish Constabulary in the "Battle of the Widow McCormack's Cabbage Patch" in County Tipperary.

△ Daniel O'Connell, creator and leader of the Catholic Association of Ireland, through which he pressed successfully for Catholic Emancipation in 1829. His failure to achieve an end to the Act of Union led many of his more militant followers to turn to violence, often with tragic results.

The effects of the famine

The Young Irelanders had not been helped by the Great Famine. Between 1845 and 1849 the potato crops failed, leading to mass starvation among the native Irish. An estimated 1.3 million people died and a further 1.4 million emigrated, chiefly to the United States. They took with them a deep hatred of the British for not doing more to help. This was soon expressed in secret societies, dedicated to Irish independence by force. In 1858 the Irish Revolutionary (later Republican) Brotherhood (IRB) and the Fenian Brotherhood were formed in New York. Together, they "invaded" Canada in 1866 and organized an uprising in Ireland a year later. Both failed.

Home Rule

Thus, by the 1860s two strands of Irish nationalism had emerged – one based on force, the other on constitutional pressure – which weave their way through modern Irish history. At first, the constitutional strand enjoyed some success, especially under the leadership of Charles Stewart Parnell. He was a Protestant-Irish politician, intent on land reform in Ireland as well as "Home Rule" – the revival of an Irish Parliament, responsible for Irish affairs. By 1907, after a series of Land Acts, most Irish farmers had been granted the "Three Fs" (fair rent, fixed tenancies and freedom to pass their tenancies onto their sons), but Home Rule proved more controversial. Two Home Rule Bills, in 1886 and 1893, failed to pass through the British parliament at Westminster, while a third was rejected by the House of Lords in 1912 and 1913.

△ The interior of a peasants' hut in Ireland during the famine of 1845-49, showing the poor living conditions and effects of starvation. Many Irish emigrated, simply to survive.

▽ Charles Stewart Parnell, the Irish Protestant politician. He was intent on land reform and the revival of an Irish parliament in Ireland (Home Rule) during the late 19th century. He had some success.

Rival forces form

However, under new legislation, the Home Rule Bill could not be rejected by the Lords a third time, so was set to become law in 1914. By then, the Irish Protestants, seeing this as the first step towards Catholic domination, had created their own armed force – the Ulster Volunteer Force (UVF) – to oppose Home Rule. This action led the nationalists to establish a rival force, the Irish Volunteers. By the summer of 1914 civil war in Ireland seemed imminent. It was only avoided by the outbreak of the First World War.

▽ British soldiers man a hastily constructed street barricade in Dublin during the Easter Uprising, in April 1916. The initial moves by the Irish nationalists on 24 April – including the seizure of the Post Office in Sackville Street – met little opposition. But a reaction from Britain was inevitable.

The Irish role in the First World War

Most Irishmen supported Britain's war against Germany – over 200,000 served in the British Army between 1914 and 1918. But a minority, chiefly members of the IRB and Irish Volunteers, saw it as an opportunity for revolt. They were led by patriots such as Patrick Pearse, Tom Clarke and Joseph Plunkett – men fired by a revival of Gaelic culture in the 1890s and dedicated to the creation of a Republic, free from British rule.

The rebels made their move on Easter Monday, 24 April 1916. They occupied a number of buildings in Dublin, including the General Post Office in Sackville (O'Connell) Street. Pearse issued a Proclamation of Irish Independence, but was forced to surrender on 29 April to superior British forces. As the surviving rebels marched into captivity, they were spat on by the very people they had tried to free.

▷ A British cavalry trooper stands guard over the remains of a nationalist barricade in Dublin in the aftermath of the Easter Uprising in 1916. The damage inflicted on the streets around the centre of Dublin, as the British deployed their forces, was significant. Yet, the ordinary people of the battle-scarred city of Dublin remained hostile to the rebels. It was not until the British began to execute rebel leaders that public opinion changed.

The two factions strengthen

But, when the British began to execute the rebel leaders, Irish opinion changed, leading to a sudden revival of the IRB, now named the Irish Republican Army (IRA). By 1919 the IRA was strong enough to begin a guerrilla campaign against the British authorities in Ireland, concentrating on the Royal Irish Constabulary (RIC) as representatives of an alien rule. By June 1920, 55 policemen had been killed and 74 wounded, forcing the British to draft in reinforcements – ex-military men known as the "Black and Tans" (from the colour of their uniforms) and Auxiliaries.

An unsuccessful solution

The British reinforcements proved difficult to control. On 21 November 1920, in response to IRA attacks against the RIC, Black and Tans and Auxiliaries fired into the crowd watching the all-Ireland Gaelic football final in Dublin. Twelve people were killed. A week later, the Black and Tans burned down the centre of Cork in retaliation to an IRA ambush in the area.

As the violence increased, the British offered a compromise. Ireland would be split, with one parliament in Dublin for the predominantly Catholic South and one in Belfast for the predominantly Protestant North. On 6 December 1921, Irish nationalist negotiators accepted the idea of an Irish Free State "faithful to HM King George V". The Protestants opted for closer ties with Britain.

Proclamation of Irish Independence, read out by Patrick Pearse in Dublin, 24 April 1916: "Irishmen and Irishwomen: In the name of God and the dead generations from which she receives her old tradition of nationhood, Ireland, through us, summons her children to her flag and strikes for her freedom....We declare the right of the people of Ireland to the ownership of Ireland, and to the unfettered control of Irish destinies...we hereby proclaim the Irish Republic as a Sovereign Independent State, and we pledge our lives...to the cause of its freedom, of its welfare, and of its exaltation among the nations." Pearse was forced to surrender in spite of this provocative proclamation but support for Irish independence continued.

Prospects for a divided land

The Free State faced a bleak future. More militant members of the IRA, led by Eamon de Valera (a hero of 1916), refused to accept anything less than complete Irish independence, and in June 1922 they occupied the Four Courts in Dublin. A Nationalist Army, raised by the Free State and commanded by Michael Collins (soon to be assassinated), put down the revolt by April 1923, but the Civil War left deep scars – that have lasted to this day. These wounds were deepened by high unemployment, a lack of industrial development (most of Ireland's industry was situated in the North) and continued emigration. The Free State government opted for conservatism, setting aside many of the social and economic reforms advocated by *Sinn Fein* and the IRA, who could offer no opposition as they refused to sit in the *Dail* (the Irish name for Parliament). Ireland began to stagnate.

△ Eamon de Valera (in the dark coat) inspects members of the IRA in 1922, at the time of the Irish Civil War. The IRA opposed the Treaty with Britain which split Ireland.

▽ The Irish delegates who signed the 1921 Treaty with Britain. On the left is Arthur Griffith, founder of the Republican political party, *Sinn Fein* ("Ourselves Alone").

In 1926 de Valera decided to create more constitutional opposition, founding a new political party – *Fianna Fail* ("Soldiers of Destiny") – and leading it into the *Dail* (Parliament). By 1932 he had formed a government which not only began to tackle economic issues but also, by a new Constitution in 1937, altered the relationship with Britain, ending the need for professed loyalty to the Crown and transforming the Free State into Eire. In 1948 Eire became a Republic, snipping the last ties with Britain. (Eire is the Gaelic term for Ireland).

The IRA re-emerges

But not everyone in the South accepted the situation. Many regarded Irish independence as incomplete so long as Northern Ireland existed. They believed in the part of the 1937 Constitution that stated that national territory was "the whole of Ireland".

The remnants of the IRA, who had gone "underground" in the aftermath of the Civil War, re-emerged to advocate violence to achieve this aim. They carried out bombing attacks in London, Birmingham, Manchester and Coventry between January and August 1939.

Governments in the South may have opposed the IRA (during the Second World War, when Eire was neutral, most IRA men were detained in the South), but to Protestants in the North, the ultimate aim of Catholic, Republican domination seemed clear.

▽ Prime Ministers Margaret Thatcher of Britain and Garret Fitzgerald of Ireland sign the 1985 Anglo-Irish Agreement in the small Northern Ireland town of Hillsborough on 15 November 1985. This was an ambitious attempt to finally resolve the differences between the people of Northern and Southern Ireland. This Agreement was signed more than 60 years after Ireland was first divided in 1921. The intervening years were full of continued unrest.

The Troubled Province

The creation of Northern Ireland in 1921, separate from the Free State in the South, was guaranteed to cause trouble. This came in 1969, when riots in the North led to a commitment of British troops. It continues still.

The North-South divide

Northern Ireland was created in 1921 when the Protestant majority in the counties of Antrim, Armagh, Down, Fermanagh, Londonderry and Tyrone voted to stay as part of the United Kingdom rather than join the Free State in the South. The border between North and South placed many Catholics outside the Free State, particularly in Armagh and Londonderry, yet denied to the Protestants what they saw as the whole of Ulster by giving the counties of Cavan, Donegal and Monaghan to the South. The new province was a compromise, satisfying no one completely.

Discrimination against Catholics

In 1921 Northern Ireland had a population of about 1.25 million, with twice as many Protestants as Catholics. The Protestants, being in the majority, used their power to suppress the Catholics, who were distrusted as agents of Irish nationalism and Republicanism. The Protestants, not unnaturally, won every general election to the Northern Ireland parliament after 1921, and every Prime Minister was a member of the Orange Order, a "Loyalist" society first founded in the 1790s. Schools were segregated along religious lines;

better jobs, particularly those in important industries such as shipbuilding, went to those who were "loyal" to the Crown; council housing was allocated more readily to Protestants, reflecting their control of local government, even in Catholic-dominated areas. In the city of Londonderry, for example, although the population in 1968 was 69 per cent Catholic, 12 out of the 20 seats on the council were held by Protestants. This blatant discrimination was achieved by "gerrymandering" – the altering of administrative boundaries to ensure Protestant majorities. Another unjust aspect of Northern Ireland voting was that only people who owned a house could vote in local elections. This gave preference to the better-off sections of the community, which, particularly in Londonderry, meant the Protestant sector of the population.

Such domination, backed by a police force (the Royal Ulster Constabulary or RUC) and its reserve (the "B" Specials) which was overwhelmingly Protestant, led to unrest, particularly in the 1960s when human rights became a political issue. In February 1967 a group of activists, drawn from both sides of the religious divide, formed the Northern Ireland Civil Rights Association (NICRA) to press for electoral reform and an end to discrimination. Marches were organized to gain publicity and in November 1968 the prime minister of Northern Ireland, Terence O'Neill, promised change.

△ A block of flats in a Catholic area of Belfast. The city has separate Catholic and Protestant areas – there is still poor housing in both.

◁ Map showing the partition of Ireland, as agreed in 1921. The border separates Northern Ireland from the Republic in the South.

Protestants resort to violence
Extreme Loyalists, convinced that NICRA was the spearhead of a Republican insurrection, responded with violence. In early January 1969 a civil rights march from Belfast to Londonderry was ambushed by Loyalists outside the village of Claudy. The RUC did not intervene.

▷ Huge dockyard cranes tower above the shipyards in the industrial part of Belfast. The twin issues of employment and housing, particularly among the suppressed Catholics, helped to fuel the civil rights crisis of 1968-69.

Violence spread to the cities, fuelled in July and August by the annual Protestant celebrations to commemorate the victories of 1690: the Battle of the Boyne that established British rule in Ireland. Catholic houses were burned down and families forced to flee. Some of them went to the South, where the Dublin government began to fear the prospect of a new civil war. Others remained in the North, attacking Protestant areas and building street barricades to protect their homes.

The RUC called in the "B" Specials, many of whom promptly aided the Protestant rioters. On 14 August 1969 the British Army was ordered onto the streets.

The British Army in Northern Ireland

The Army's role at this stage was one of peacekeeping – calming the situation by keeping the two sides apart. At first, many Catholics welcomed the soldiers, offering cups of tea and dismantling the barricades.

Yet, in a matter of months all this had changed. Some people blamed the Army for using heavy-handed tactics, culminating in an incident in Londonderry on 30 January 1972 known as "Bloody Sunday". It was on this day that 13 civilians were shot dead by British Army soldiers. Other people argued that the Army merely reacted to increased violence which developed as the situation was exploited by Republican groups, notably the IRA, who saw it as an opportunity for political gain. The latter seems closer to the truth. However, in the prevailing situation of distrust and religious division, opinion will always vary, reflecting beliefs.

The Role of the Army
Initially deployed as a peacekeeping force, the British Army in Northern Ireland soon assumed the role of containing extremist violence, especially in Londonderry and Belfast, in South Armagh and along the border. At the height of the most recent "troubles" in 1972, up to 17,000 British troops were stationed in the province, patrolling, reacting to violence and gathering intelligence, all "in aid of the civil power". This figure has now been reduced to about 10,000.

▽ A British soldier, armed and wearing a protective helmet, talks to a young Northern Irish boy, fascinated by the instruments of war. The boy is growing up in an atmosphere of violence.

A crisis develops

In 1969, the IRA was weak. A military campaign on the border between 1956 and 1962 had failed, and in its aftermath the group had adopted a more political approach, seeking to create a National Liberation Front with other fringe parties. In January 1970 activists from Northern Ireland, led by Ruari O'Bradaigh and Sean MacStiofain, broke away to form the Provisional IRA (PIRA).

This new faction of the IRA was determined to use violence to force the British out and to prepare the way for an all-Ireland socialist Republic. Using Catholic areas as "safe bases" and the "excesses" of the British Army as proof of Protestant oppression, they began to gain support from a cross-section of the Catholic society. On 6 February 1971, they killed their first British soldier.

Resentment and internment

The government response, introduced on 9 August 1971, was to arrest known IRA suspects and to put them in prison without the benefit of a trial – a process known as "internment". As no Protestants were arrested, this further alienated the Catholics, who began to see the Army as an instrument of the existing system. Barricades were rebuilt and "No-Go" areas created in Belfast and Londonderry to keep the soldiers out. The violence spread, made worse by Protestant groups such as the Ulster Volunteer Force and Red Hand Commandos, whose extremist members, imbued with the hatred of generations, attacked the Republicans.

▽ The scene in Londonderry on Sunday, 30 January 1972, as a massive crowd, protesting about the lack of civil rights in Northern Ireland, approaches a British Army barricade. When a minority in the crowd began to take a more violent attitude, the Army reacted. There was bloodshed, and by the end of the day, 13 civilians were dead.

Unsuccessful solutions

What was needed was a political initiative, putting forward universally acceptable solutions to the problems of Northern Ireland. This could not come from a Northern Ireland Parliament which clearly enjoyed little Catholic support, so on 24 March 1972 direct rule from London was imposed. Four months later, the Army occupied the "No-Go" areas.

A political initiative emerged in 1973, based on "power sharing", in which legitimate Catholic political parties would be guaranteed a voice in the government of the province. It was destroyed by a general strike, organized by

▽ A Royal Ulster Constabulary (RUC) Landrover edges past a street barricade in Belfast in the aftermath of a riot. Street riots have been a characteristic of the present "troubles", often being used as cover for extremist gunmen intent on killing members of the police or Army.

the Loyalist-backed Ulster Workers' Council, in May 1974, leaving Northern Ireland in a political vacuum.

Until fresh ideas could be worked out, it was up to the Security Forces (the Army and RUC) to contain the violence. The aim was to create an atmosphere that was free from the emotions of extremism in which political solutions could be calmly discussed. In this, the Security Forces were aided by the extremists themselves, who alienated many of their own supporters.

When IRA bombs exploded in two Birmingham public houses on 21 November 1974, for example, killing 19 people, there was widespread public disgust. This allowed the government to introduce tougher "anti-terrorism" laws and to replace internment by policies which treated convicted gunmen and bombers, Protestant as well as Catholic, as common criminals.

Birmingham Bombs
On the evening of 21 November 1974, IRA activists planted bombs in two public houses in the centre of Birmingham: the *Tavern in the Town* and the *Mulberry Bush*.

Attempts to give warnings failed and 21 innocent people were killed. Six Irishmen were convicted of the outrage, but strong doubts have been expressed about their guilt. They are still in prison.

△ Women in Northern Ireland – members of the Peace People, formerly the Women's Peace Movement (top) protest outside Belfast Town Hall in 1977. Mairead Farrell (above) a leading member of the Provisional IRA, shot dead by a special branch of the British Army, the SAS, in Gibraltar, near Spain, in March 1988.

The Women's Peace Movement

Other incidents seemed to suggest that people were turning away from the extremist groups. On 10 August 1976 three children were accidentally killed when an IRA getaway car, being chased by the Army, crashed in Belfast. The children's aunt, Mairead Corrigan, and her friend Betty Williams founded the Women's Peace Movement (later renamed the Peace People) and received substantial support from ordinary folk on both sides of the religious divide. Mass peace rallies were held in Belfast and elsewhere.

By late 1977 the movement had begun to fade, but its success (marked by the award of the Nobel Peace Prize to Corrigan and Williams in 1977) undermined much of the support previously given to the extremists, particularly the IRA. When this coincided with increased Security Force effectiveness – indicated by a significant drop in the number of deaths from extremist action and by a new policy (known as "Ulsterization") which transferred many security duties back to the RUC – the IRA seemed close to defeat. Internal feuding between Republican groups did little to strengthen their cause, diverting energies away from fighting British rule.

The fighting continues

The Provisionals in the North, led now by Gerry Adams and Martin McGuinness, responded by reorganizing their depleted ranks, moving away from the old structure of "brigades" and "battalions" and towards a much tighter "cellular" structure of dedicated, experienced activists.

A "cell" would typically comprise a quartermaster, who looked after the weapons and explosives, an intelligence expert, a bomb-maker and a gunman, who would come together for a particular attack and then disperse, probably without knowing the names of constituent members. Thus, if one of the activists was captured, he would be unable to tell the Security Forces anything of value.

The new IRA received money and weapons from a variety of sources. In the United States, the Irish Northern Aid Committee (Noraid) was strongly suspected of channelling funds to the extremists, while on a more international, non-Irish, level, the Libyan leader Colonel Gadaffi provided substantial shipments of arms.

▷ The funeral of IRA hunger-striker, Bobby Sands, May 1981: an occasion for Republican mourning and renewed confrontation. Sands died on the 66th day without food and his action was followed by other hunger strikers. A further nine died between May and August 1981 before these tactics were called off.

▽ A British soldier, wearing helmet and vizor, in case of riots, and armed with an SA 80 rifle, on the streets of Belfast, 1988. His presence raises no protest from passers-by.

▽ The notorious "H-blocks" in the Maze prison, Belfast, built in the late 1970s to house extremists found guilty of "terrorist" crimes once internment had ended. The "H-blocks" were the scene of the Republican prisoners' protests and hunger strikes of 1980-81. They wanted better prison conditions and political status. There was widespread Catholic support for the strikers.

Certainly, the IRA was showing its new potential as early as 27 August 1979, when Earl Mountbatten was murdered; on the same day 18 soldiers were killed at Warrenpoint in County Down.

Imprisonment and hunger strikes
But the British refused to be intimidated and, as the Security Forces concentrated on low-level intelligence gathering and deployed the experts of the Special Air Service (SAS) Regiment, many extremists found themselves facing long prison sentences in the specially built "H-blocks" of the Maze prison, outside Belfast.

They refused to wear prison clothes (known as going "on the blanket", as that was all they had to wear) or to clean their cells (known as the "dirty protest"). For several years IRA and other Republican prisoners wore blankets only, rather than accept prison uniform and they refused to co-operate with the prison regime. Then in late 1980, there was a series of hunger strikes. When Bobby Sands died on 5 May 1981 – the first of ten Republicans to starve themselves to death – there were riots in the streets and the IRA seemed to regain support. This had been shown most forcibly in April 1981 when Bobby Sands, despite his criminal status, was elected MP for Fermanagh and South Tyrone in the Westminster parliament, London.

Sinn Fein in politics

This proved to be a turning-point in the history of the IRA. In the light of Sands' success, Adams initiated a move to involve the IRA in more political activities. It was a dangerous ploy, bearing in mind the number of times the IRA had been split by similar political activities in the past. But Adams introduced his new ideas carefully.

At the 1981 *ard fheis* (annual meeting) Adams' ally, Danny Morrison, stood up and asked, "Who here really believes that we can win the war through the ballot-box? But will anyone here object if with a ballot paper in this hand and an Armalite (a US-manufactured rifle much favoured by the Provisionals) in this hand we take power in Ireland?" Using the Republican organization *Sinn Fein* as a political mouthpiece, the strategy enjoyed some success.

In 1982 elections were held in Northern Ireland to an Assembly of 78 members who would gradually assume

△ Members of the Provisional IRA, complete with handguns and distinctive black balaclavas, pose for a propaganda picture in the back streets of Belfast.

◁ A street mural (far left) on the provocatively named RPG (rocket-propelled grenade) Avenue. It shows the Spirit of Ireland offering freedom from the ills of British rule – housing, jobs, culture and oppression.

◁ Gerry Adams, President of the Provisional *Sinn Fein*. He is a Republican, representing West Belfast in parliament since 1983. He advocates a mixture of political activity and military action to try to force the British to leave Northern Ireland.

political powers. *Sinn Fein* won five seats under the prevailing process of proportional representation. At the same time, many *Sinn Fein* activists were elected onto local councils throughout Northern Ireland, representing Catholic areas. They began to gain a reputation for caring about local issues and for pursuing social justice.

But this support did not grow – in the 1984 elections to the European parliament, few votes were gained – while continued military actions, such as the bombing of the Grand Hotel in Brighton in October 1984, alienated more moderate public opinion. To the majority of Catholics in the North, the IRA was still a "terrorist" organization.

This view was substantiated by several "finds" of IRA armaments. On 30 October 1987, for example, French police and customs officials seized a ship called the *Eksund* and found that it was packed with Soviet-built weapons, including launchers for SA-7 surface-to-air missiles, en route from Tripoli to the IRA. It was widely suspected that this was only one of a series of similar shipments, dating back to the 1970s. It was from this time onwards that the IRA had been suspected of receiving foreign aid.

A stalemate situation

Thus by 1984, after 15 years of violence, the crisis in Northern Ireland appeared to have settled into a stalemate. The Security Forces, despite adopting heavy-handed tactics on occasion in the early years, had learnt from their mistakes. They now concentrated on containing the situation.

The British government had an unremitting resolve not to allow the extremists to win. Also, its politico-military response was designed to isolate the activists on both sides of the religious divide. This combination of approach meant that the British were maintaining their presence in the North.

At the same time, however, the extremist groups were still active, showing a continuing capability to mount "spectaculars" which grabbed public attention for their cause. In the case of the *Sinn Fein*/IRA alliance, moreover, a degree of public support in political terms had become apparent and could not be ignored. A new government initiative, designed to exploit Security Force success and isolate the extremists entirely, was urgently needed. It came in November 1985 with the Anglo-Irish Agreement. This was an attempt by Britain to find a way of ending the conflict in Northern Ireland by constitutional means.

What May Be Done?

Northern Ireland's problems must be solved by peaceful, political means. The Anglo-Irish Agreement of November 1985 offers hope of a settlement, but a lot of work still needs to be done. The final outcome is as yet unclear.

All previous political initiatives had been based on the internal government of Northern Ireland. There was the abortive power sharing idea of 1973-74. (Power sharing was an attempt to give the nationalist community some limited but direct role in Northern Ireland's government). Equally unsuccessful was the Assembly of 1982. Now the key to the new political initiative was seen as co-operation between the British and Irish governments. The aim was to deny support to the IRA on both sides of the border, while offering the possibility of a peaceful settlement to the problems of the North. It was an idea explored as early as 1980, when the two Prime Ministers – Margaret Thatcher and Charles Haughey – met to establish "joint studies" in economic and security matters. They met to try to find a way to end the conflict and to secure peace within the province.

A year later – by which time Haughey had been replaced by Garret Fitzgerald – the process was taken further, with the creation of an Anglo-Irish Intergovernmental Council, within which representatives of both countries could discuss Northern Ireland and its future. It was the first time the Republic had been given a voice (albeit a relatively minor one) in the affairs of the North.

Attempts to promote peace

After further negotiations, a full-scale Anglo-Irish Agreement was signed at Hillsborough, outside Belfast, on 15 November 1985, designed to "promote peace and stability in Northern Ireland". The role of the Republic was more closely defined, allowing the Dublin government to "put forward views and proposals relating to Northern Ireland", principally in terms of security, justice and politics. In exchange, the Republic agreed to accept the existing division of Ireland, so long as the majority in the North desired it. The Agreement sought to recognize and respect the identities of the two communities in Northern Ireland and the right of each to pursue its aspirations by peaceful and constitutional means. The Republic effectively dropped the controversial clause in the 1937 Constitution claiming national territory to be "the whole of Ireland".

Despite some of the conditions – clearly designed to ease the fears of Protestants in the North – the effects of the Anglo-Irish Agreement were mixed. Many Loyalists saw it as merely a device "to trundle Northern Ireland into an All-Ireland Republic", but their "Day of Action" on 3 March 1986, designed to try to recreate the paralysis of the Ulster Workers' Council Strike 12 years earlier, did not receive the support expected. After nearly 20 years of violence, too many people – Protestant and Catholic alike – were prepared to give the Agreement a chance to work.

This enabled the two governments to start building up mutual confidence, exploring the realities of their professed co-operation. The process was not easy, but some success was slowly achieved. Border security, for example, was improved as forces in the North worked in conjunction with the *Garda* (police) and Army in the South. For, although local difficulties could arise, the use of the Republic by the IRA as a "safe haven" began to be curtailed. This was backed up by an Extradition Treaty, whereby extremists arrested in the Republic could be transferred to the North (or vice versa) if wanted for questioning there. Again, it took time to set this up, but by 1989 a number of men wanted for crimes in the North had been transferred in this way.

◁ Ulster Loyalists protest about the terms of the Anglo-Irish Agreement, signed at Hillsborough, Belfast, in November 1985. Some of the more militant Protestants feel that the Agreement attempts to undermine Protestant privileges in Northern Ireland – which is partly true.

Future possibilities

However, regardless of the hopes attached to it, the Anglo-Irish Agreement can never produce a solution. All it can do is to provide a base from which long-term solutions may emerge. By offering alternatives to the extremist policies of violence, a more rational discussion on the future of the North may come about.

What that future will be has yet to be decided. The British government, despite Protestant fears, has shown no intention of relinquishing control of the North, so there is every indication that it will remain as part of the United Kingdom.

At the same time, however, its links, both economic and

◁ Mourners gather for the funeral of IRA Volunteer Kevin McCracken in Belfast, 1988. Such occasions are used to reaffirm the loyalties of Republican sympathizers. They are emotive scenes that can inspire violence.

The SAS in Gibraltar
On Sunday, 6 March 1988, three IRA activists – Mairead Farrell, Daniel McCann and Sean Savage – crossed the border from Spain into the British colony of Gibraltar. Savage parked a car – a white Renault 5 – close to the governor's residence, where a British Army band would halt during the changing of the guard the following Tuesday.

Convinced that the car contained a bomb which could be detonated by remote control, members of the Special Air Service (SAS) Regiment, who had been tasked to watch the three IRA suspects, closed in, aiming to make arrests.

When Farrell and McCann were confronted, they made movements which were construed to be hostile and were shot. Savage, some distance away, started to run when he heard the shots, was challenged and also killed. In the event, the car did not contain explosives (they were still in Spain), but the intentions of the IRA team were never denied.

△ Gerard Kelly, an IRA fugitive, at a hearing in Dublin, Southern Ireland, on a British request for his extradition. The Anglo-Irish Agreement depends on the willingness of each government to co-operate like this.

political, are likely to be strengthened with the Republic, gradually undermining some of the politico-religious suspicions that have prevented co-operation in the past. This implies that, in the long term, a reunification of Ireland, based on calm and open debate rather than bombs or bullets, could be a possibility. Alternatively, Northern Ireland could emerge as an independent state in its own right. Only time will tell.

Meanwhile, the Security Forces of both North and South must continue to work to reduce the levels of violence, avoiding, if at all possible, outrages such as Enniskillen. It will all take time – the IRA, for example, is still a potent force, quite capable of carrying out attacks in Europe as well as in Northern Ireland and Britain. Any lapse in security could undermine much of the work so laboriously done so far. The best that may be said is that the Anglo-Irish Agreement could be a faint glimmer of light at the end of a long and wearisome tunnel. The beginnings of that tunnel lie over 800 years in the past, defying us to understand and resolve.

▽ A British soldier mans a vehicle checkpoint close to the border between North and South Ireland. Although the Dublin Government has a long tradition of opposing the IRA, they can do little to prevent the extremists from using the Republic (Southern Ireland) as a "safe haven". The Anglo-Irish Agreement of 1985 addressed this problem and cross-border security co-operation was created.

There have been numerous deaths, injuries and bombings in Northern Ireland connected with the conflicting political situation. Since 1969 there have been over 2,800 deaths and 26,000 people have been injured, many very seriously. Civil rights, censorship and mistreatment of suspected extremists has left a legacy of bitterness that could last for generations.

Irish Northern Aid Committee (Noraid) Founded in the United States in 1969 by three elderly Republicans – Michael Flannery, John McCarthy, and John MacGowan – specifically for raising money among Irish-Americans to provide relief to victims of the "troubles" in Northern Ireland.

In reality, this relief was offered only to Catholics and to the families of IRA men who had been either killed or imprisoned by the British. Suspicion quickly grew that a substantial part of the money raised went on the purchase of arms and explosives, which was not a popular cause.

Although still active, Noraid's influence has been undermined by the United States. This has been done through actions such as the infiltration of the Noraid organization by the Federal Bureau of Investigation (FBI).

Irish Republican Army (IRA) Formed in 1916 at the time of the Easter Uprising, but with roots in earlier Republican and anti-British organizations, notably the Irish Revolutionary (later Republican) Brotherhood (IRB), founded in 1858.

The IRA was largely responsible for conducting a successful guerrilla campaign against the British between 1919 and 1921. They concentrated their attacks against the Royal Irish Constabulary and Army that were seen as being representative of British rule.

However, the more militant members of the group refused to accept the Treaty with Britain, made in 1921, which partitioned the country of Ireland into the North and the South. At this time, the country was uneven in its economic development. The Catholic South was more rural and poorer than the North. The IRA dedicated themselves to the reunification of the island of Ireland by force.

The IRA was defeated in the Irish Civil War (1922-23), and was further weakened by Eamon de Valera's decision to follow a more political line in

▽ **Emigration from Ireland**
For well over a century, emigration has been part of life in Ireland. For some people, leaving and going abroad was the only way to escape the poverty and hunger of 19th century Ireland. At the height of the famine, in 1849, people were leaving from every port in Ireland. Most went to the United States, where they hoped to make a fresh start.

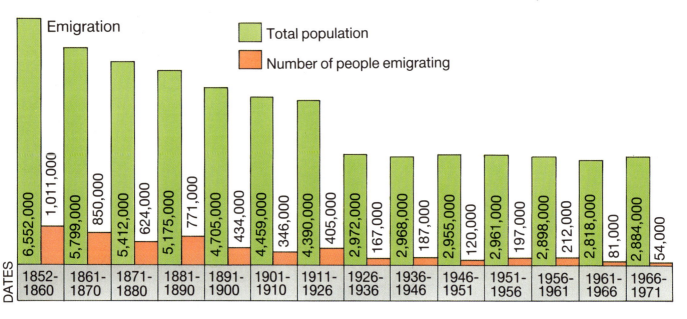

Emigration

■ Total population
■ Number of people emigrating

DATES	1852-1860	1861-1870	1871-1880	1881-1890	1891-1900	1901-1910	1911-1926	1926-1936	1936-1946	1946-1951	1951-1956	1956-1961	1961-1966	1966-1971
Total population	6,552,000	5,799,000	5,412,000	5,175,000	4,705,000	4,459,000	4,390,000	2,972,000	2,968,000	2,955,000	2,961,000	2,898,000	2,818,000	2,884,000
Number of people emigrating	1,011,000	850,000	624,000	771,000	434,000	346,000	405,000	167,000	187,000	120,000	197,000	212,000	81,000	54,000

. . and Violence

YEAR	RUC		ARMY		CIVILIANS	
	Killed	Wounded	Killed	Wounded	Killed	Wounded
1969	1	8		24	12	139
1970	2	47		620	23	60
1971	11	105	48	390	115	1880
1972	17	94	129	578	321	3902
1973	13	94	66	548	171	1765
1974	15	59	35	483	166	1394
1975	11	79	20	167	216	1213
1976	23	74	29	264	245	1087
1977	14	51	29	187	69	406
1978	10	174	21	135	50	253
1979	14	117	48	153	51	305
1980	9	136	17	77	50	266
1981	21	219	23	140	67	433
1982	12	81	28	98	57	256
1983	18	110	15	88	44	202
1984	8	189	19	86	37	252
1985	23	305	6	31	24	245
1986	12	417	12	55	38	322
1987 *	9	39	4	44	29	137
TOTAL	243	2398	549	4168	1785	14517

* Detailed break down not available after May 1987

◁ **Violence in Northern Ireland** The figures on the left show the number of people – among the Royal Ulster Constabulary (RUC), Army and civilians – killed and wounded between August 1969 and May 1987. The nature and the scale of violence has fluctuated. The peak was in 1972 when fighting between the IRA and the British Army was at its most intense and Loyalist groups were at their most active in killing Catholic civilians. Since 1972 the scale of violence has decreased and during the 1980s the death toll averaged around 76 a year. Recently there have been relatively few British Army casualties.

1926. Despite campaigns against the British in 1939 and 1956-62, the IRA remained a peripheral organization.

By 1969, the leaders of the IRA, based in Dublin, in the South of Ireland, were again exploring the possibility of political rather than violent action. This left the existing IRA unable to respond to the new round of troubles in the North. As a result, in late 1969, the IRA split into two factions, which emerged in January 1970 as the Official IRA (OIRA) and the Provisional IRA (PIRA).

Official Irish Republican Army (OIRA) Based in Dublin, it continued to follow a more political approach, although it has on occasions felt obliged to use violence.

OIRA bomb that killed seven people in the Parachute Regiment Officers' Mess in Aldershot. However, in May 1972 the OIRA declared an indefinite ceasefire which has been maintained since that date.

The professed aim of the OIRA is "revolutionary socialism" – the bringing together of all workers (Protestant and Catholic) in Ireland to sweep existing governments away.

Provisional Irish Republican Army (PIRA) Comprising the more militant Republicans, chiefly in the North, who felt that a political approach was unlikely to succeed. This faction of the IRA took immediate advantage of the deployment of the British Army in Belfast. Led initially by Ruari O'Bradaigh and Sean MacStiofain, it enjoyed

some success against the British in the early 1970s, escalating the conflict in Ireland and spreading its impact to the mainland with selective bomb attacks.

By 1976-77, however, many of the PIRA leaders had been arrested, discredited or killed, leading to a reorganization into a "cellular" structure of dedicated fighters which the Security Forces found difficult to break.

Nevertheless, the PIRA's involvement in sectarian and factional fighting, coupled with increased Security Force expertise, weakened the PIRA's effects. In the aftermath of the hunger strikes in 1981, Gerry Adams initiated moves to involve the PIRA in politics, using *Sinn Fein* as the mouthpiece. This has not prevented acts of violence.

Extremist Organizations. . . . .

Irish Republican Socialist Party (IRSP) Formed in December 1974 when more militant members of the Official IRA, tired of the lack of action, broke away.

Within months, the IRSP had created its own force, the Irish National Liberation Army (INLA), which has been responsible for sectarian murders and, most notably, the assassination of Airey Neave MP, Conservative Party spokesman on Northern Ireland, in March 1979.

Red Hand Commandos
Formed as an offshoot of the Ulster Defence Association (UDA) in Belfast in mid-1972. Its members – drawn from the more extreme elements of the Loyalist community – were notorious for their sectarian violence. They ceased to be effective after the assassination of their leader, John McKeague, in 1982.

***Sinn Fein* ("Ourselves Alone")**
The original Irish Nationalist Party, founded in 1905, traditionally associated with the IRA. It split into Official and Provisional wings with the IRA, acting as a political "front" organization in both cases. The Provisional wing has become more prominent since the early 1980s, as the "ballot box and Armalite" strategy of PIRA developed.

This strategy arose from the idea that appeared in the *Sinn Fein* newspaper *An Phoblacht* that "the essence of the Republican struggle must be in armed resistance coupled with popular opposition to the British presence. So, while not everyone can plant a bomb, everyone can plant a vote". This kind of simplistic message was appealing to many people in the early 1980s. The attitude tended to be suppressed by the popular media, particularly television.

Ulster Defence Association (UDA) Formed among extreme Loyalists in Belfast in 1971 in an attempt to bring together a host of local anti-Republican groups. Its aim is to oppose the IRA using similar tactics of violence, but it has always been faction-driven and subject to splits.

Despite a declared membership of 60,000 in 1973 and a reputation for public displays of force, the UDA has tended to be used as an "umbrella" by a number of more violent groups involved in sectarian attacks. The UDA is basically a Protestant paramilitary organization, without a political wing. It does not accept the Anglo-Irish Agreement.

Ulster Freedom Fighters (UFF) Emerged in 1973 as an offshoot of the UDA. Its membership consisted of extremist Loyalists, intent on using violence across the sectarian divide, provoking IRA retaliation and creating confrontation.

UFF members have been responsible for a number of attacks against Republicans, including, in March 1984, an attempted assassination of Gerry Adams, President of Provisional *Sinn Fein*.

Sinn Fein and Social Democratic and Labour Party electoral statistics (as percentages) 1982-87

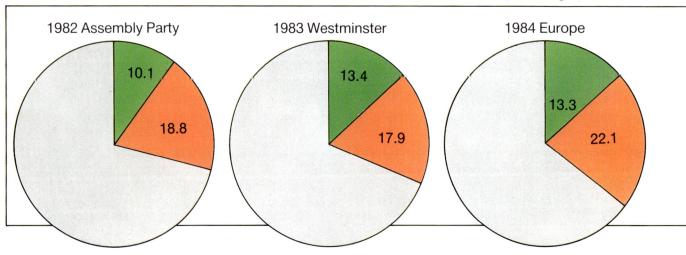

■ *Sinn Fein*
■ Social Democratic and Labour Party

1982 Assembly Party — 10.1 / 18.8

1983 Westminster — 13.4 / 17.9

1984 Europe — 13.3 / 22.1

. . and Politics

Ulster Volunteer Force (UVF)
Successor to the UVF which was first formed in 1912-1914. It had the support of many leading British conservative politicians at that time. The modern UVF was re-formed in 1966 by "Gusty" Spence as a "military body dedicated to upholding the constitution of Ulster by force if necessary".

It has been responsible for a number of sectarian murders, but its power was largely broken in 1976-77 by the arrest, trial and conviction of its leaders.

LEGITIMATE PARTIES

Social Democratic and Labour Party (SDLP) The most successful political party that represents the Catholic minority. It was formed in the early 1970s, partly as a political response to the success and enthusiasm of the civil rights movement of the time.

The original main objectives of the SDLP were to organize and maintain a Socialist Party in Northern Ireland and to promote the idea of Irish unity on behalf of the Catholic people. Unlike *Sinn Fein*, the SDLP does not believe in an armed struggle. However, it is a nationalistic party. Prior to 1969 nationalistic parties in Ireland tended to have affiliations with *Sinn Fein*. But, contrary to traditional practices relations between *Sinn Fein* and the SDLP have always been competitive rather than amicable and conciliatory.

Democratic Unionist Party (DUP) Formed in 1971 to represent Irish Protestants with the Reverend Ian Paisley as its dominant spokesman.

Ulster Unionist Party (UUP)
Formed to fight against Home Rule. The UUP represents the Protestants. From 1920 to 1972 the UUP has been well represented in Britain at Westminster. In the past it has enjoyed good relations with the British Conservative Party and during the 1970s had the support of MP Enoch Powell – an outstanding parliamentarian. The party philosophy is the desire for Ireland to be integrated into the British system in the same way as Scotland and Wales.

A harsh political climate
Northern Ireland's party system is different from that of any other Western nation. Some people feel it has, in the past, had more resemblance to the political system of a Latin American country, where military and foreign involvement in politics are taken for granted.

A comparison of *Sinn Fein* and Social Democratic and Labour Party (SDLP) election results 1982-87.
Catholic politics is reflected by the election results below. The mainstream Catholic political party, the SDLP enjoyed a virtually unchallenged position within the Catholic community, until the hunger strikes of 1981. But, the SDLP remained popular because it changed its tactics – meeting challenges posed both by *Sinn Fein* and developments in Anglo-Irish relations – and so managed to maintain its stronghold within the nationalistic community.

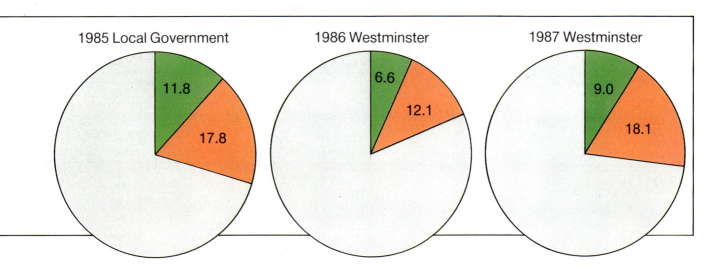

1985 Local Government · 11.8 · 17.8

1986 Westminster · 6.6 · 12.1

1987 Westminster · 9.0 · 18.1

Chronology

The population of Ireland
About 5 million live in Ireland. Of these about 3.5 million people live in the Republic (in the South) and 93 per cent of them are Catholics. Of the 1.5 million people living in Northern Ireland, 60 per cent are Protestant and most of the rest are Catholic. The different experiences between these two religious groups and their segregation has led to problems in Ireland.

1169 Richard FitzGilbert de Clare ("Strongbow") arrives in Ireland

1595 Rebellion by Hugh O'Neill of Ulster

1609 "Plantation" of Ulster begins

1641 Catholic rebellion; 12,000 "planters" massacred

1649 Oliver Cromwell arrives in Ireland to impose British Rule by terror

1688-89 Seige of Londonderry denies the city to James II

1690 Battle of the Boyne won by William of Orange (July)

1796 Orange Order of "Loyalists" founded

1798 Wolfe Tone rebellion put down by the British

1801 Act of Union enforced (January); Irish Parliament disbanded, Ireland ruled from London as part of a "United Kingdom"

1803 Rebellion led by Robert Emmet fails

1829 Catholic Emancipation granted

1845-49 The "Great Famine"; 1.3 million Irish die, 1.4 million emigrate

1848 "Battle of the Widow McCormack's Cabbage Patch"

1858 Irish Revolutionary Brotherhood (IRB) and Fenian Brotherhood formed

1867 Abortive "Fenian" uprising in Ireland

1886 First Home Rule Bill fails

1893 Second Home Rule Bill fails

1912-14 Crisis as Third Home Rule Bill succeeds. Protestants and Catholics in Ireland create rival armed forces. Civil war is averted by the outbreak of the First World War (August 1914)

1916 Easter Uprising in Dublin. Proclamation of Irish Independence and surrender of rebels (April). British execution of ringleaders alienates Irish opinion

1919-21 Irish Republican Army (IRA) guerrilla campaign against the British leads to truce and treaty to partition Ireland

1921 Ireland split into a Free State in the South, ruled from Dublin, and Northern Ireland, ruled from Belfast but still part of Great Britain

1922-23 Irish Civil War as IRA refuses to accept the Treaty

1926 Eamon de Valera forms Fianna Fail party and enters the Dail (Parliament)

1932 De Valera forms a new government of the Free State

1937 New constitution renames the Free State as Eire

1939 IRA bombing campaign in British cities

1948 Eire becomes a Republic, severing ties with Britain

1956-62 IRA campaign on the border between the Republic and the North

1967 Northern Ireland Civil Rights Association formed

1969 Riots in Londonderry and Belfast. RUC and "B" Specials overwhelmed and British Army deployed (August)

1970 IRA split into Official and Provisional wings

1971 First British soldier killed in the "troubles" that began in 1969

1972 "Bloody Sunday". British soldiers kill 13 civilians in Londonderry (January); Northern Ireland Parliament dissolved and Direct Rule from Westminster introduced

1973 "Power sharing" initiative

1974 Birmingham pub bombs

Glossary

1976 Women's Peace Movement/Peace People formed

1978 Republican prisoners in the Maze begin "dirty protest"

1979 Earl Mountbatten murdered by the IRA; 18 British soldiers killed in an IRA ambush at Warrenpoint

1980 Anglo-Irish Summit – Margaret Thatcher and Charles Haughey set up "joint studies" on security and co-operation (May). Hunger strikes begin among Republican prisoners in the Maze (October)

1981 Hunger striker Bobby Sands elected MP for Fermanagh and South Tyrone (April), then dies of self-imposed starvation (May); nine more Republicans die (May-August)

1982 Bomb explosions in Regent's Park and Hyde Park, London (July)

1983 Bomb attack on Harrods department store, London (December)

1984 Bombing of the Grand Hotel, Brighton (October) during the Conservative party conference

1985 Anglo-Irish Agreement signed at Hillsborough, Belfast (November)

1987 Remembrance Sunday bomb in Enniskillen (November)

1988 SAS shoot three IRA members in Gibraltar; two British Army corporals' murdered in Belfast (March)

Civil Rights Fair and equal treatment of all people in having jobs, homes and the right to vote.

Dail The Parliament of the Republic of Ireland.

Direct Rule Since 1972 Northern Ireland has been ruled directly from Britain.

Eire A Gaelic term for Ireland. It is more commonly used by people in Northern Ireland who are strongly opposed to a United Ireland as it makes the Republic sound foreign.

Free State Legal name of the Republic until 1948. A term often used by both Catholics and Protestants in Northern Ireland, but rarely by people in the Republic.

Home Rule The wish to give Ireland self-government.

Loyalists Irish Protestants who support the union with the United Kingdom. Broadly speaking, Loyalists are the more militant Unionists – those more willing to use force. They are loyal to the Royal Family.

Nationalists A wide range of people who all share a desire to see a united Ireland. Most of the Catholics want Northern Ireland and the Republic of Ireland to be united into one national state. Nationalists are often called Republicans. In general terms Republicans are more militant nationalists and more willing to use physical force.

Northern Ireland A neutral term for the territory north of the border.

Orange Order Society formed in 1796 to protect Protestants from Catholics. Named after William of Orange.

Planters Settlers that were sent over to Ireland, from Britain in the 17th century. They were half-English and half-Scots. By 1622 there were 22,000 of them.

Republic of Ireland The territory south of the border.

Republicans People who wish to see the two parts of Ireland joined again and independent of Britain. They have more radical social policies than nationalists.

Royal Ulster Constabulary (RUC) The police force of Northern Ireland.

Ulster This province is partly north and partly south of the border. Unionists often use the name "Ulster" to refer to Northern Ireland alone. Ulster includes three counties now in the Republic of Ireland.

Unionists A wide range of people, mostly Protestants of Northern Ireland, who all share a desire to remain legally united with Britain. They also describe themselves as being loyal to the Royal Family.

United Kingdom Great Britain (England, Scotland and Wales) plus Northern Ireland. A term often used by Unionists to emphasize the constitutional relationship between Britain and Northern Ireland. Nationalists rarely use it because it is the legal name for Great Britain and Northern Ireland together.

35

Index

Photographic credits

Cover and pages 2-3, 5, 18, 24l and r and back cover: Frank Spooner Agency; page 4-5: Doran/Network; pages 4, 8-9, 15 and 17: Sturrock/Network; pages 6l, 12, 14t, 19 and 29t: Popperfoto; pages 6r and 28: Abrahams/Network; pages 7, 8 and 11t: Mansell Collection; pages 9, 10, 11b, 13 and 14b: Mary Evans Library; page 16: Rex Features; pages 20 and 26-27: Golestan/Network; pages 21b, 22-23 and 29b: Nangle/Network; page 22: Topham Picture Library; page 23: Arkwell/Network; page 24-25: Network.